UNCOVERING THE PAST:
ANALYZING PRIMARY SOURCES

THE
CIVIL WAR

WITHDRAWN

MEGAN KOPP

CRABTREE
PUBLISHING COMPANY
WWW.CRABTREEBOOKS.COM

Author: Megan Kopp

Editor-in-Chief: Lionel Bender

Editors: Simon Adams, Ellen Rodger

Proofreaders: Laura Booth, Angela Kaelberer

Project coordinator: Petrice Custance

Design and photo research: Ben White

Production: Kim Richardson

**Production coordinator and
  prepress technician:** Ken Wright

Print coordinator: Katherine Berti

Consultants: Amie Wright, Emily Drew
  The New York Public Library

Produced for Crabtree Publishing Company
by Bender Richardson White

Photographs and reproductions:
Alamy: Front cover, 11 Btm (PF-(usna)), 15 (The Granger Collection); 8–9 Getty
Images (Buyenlarge), 13 (De Agostini Picture Library), 27 (Archive Photos) ,37 Btm
(Archive Photos), 38–39 (Universal History Archive), 40–41 Top (Siouxsnapp /
Shutterstock.com) , 40–41 Btm (Getty Images News); Library of Congress: 1 (LC-DIG-
stereo-1s02416), 3 (LC-DIG-pga-01844), Top Left (Icon) 4, 6 (LC-DIG-stereo-1s02760),
4–5 (LC-DIG-ppmsca-07636), 5 (LC-DIG-ppmsca-10974), 6 (LC-DIG-stereo-51551), 7
(LC-DIG-stereo-1s04355), Top Left (Icon) 8, 10, 12, 14 (LC-DIG-ppmsca-33443), 11 Top
(LC-DIG-ppmsca-31723), 11 Middle (LC-DIG-ppmsca-26466), 12 (LC-USZ62-93015),
Top Left (Icon) 16, 18 (LC-DIG-highsm-12732), 16–17 (LC-DIG-ppmsca-34483), 19 Top
LC-DIG-ppmsca-21066 19 Btm (LC-DIG-pga-01846), Top Left (Icon) 20, 22, 24, 26, 28,
30 (LC-DIG-ppmsca-22982), 24 (LC-DIG-ds-05202), 25 Left (LC-DIG-ppmsca-32800), 26
(LC-DIG-ppmsca-31277), 28–29 (LC-DIG-ppmsca-35548), 30–31 (LC-DIG-ppmsca-21722),
Top Left (Icon) 32, 34, 36 Everett Historical, 33 Top (LC-DIG-highsm-04713), 36 (LC-
USZ62-97173), Top Left (Icon) 38, 40 (LC-DIG-highsm-28900), 34 Btm (Mark Carell);
Topfoto: 14 (World History Archive), 18, 23, 25 Right, 32–33 (The Granger Collection),
20–21 (Ullsteinbild), 30 (The Image Works), 34 Top (HIP), 37 Top Penguin Random
House, LLC, New York

Map: Stefan Chabluk

Cover: General Sherman at Kenesaw Mountain during the Battle of Allatoona Pass
October 4 1864

Library and Archives Canada Cataloguing in Publication

Kopp, Megan, author
    The Civil War / Megan Kopp.

(Uncovering the past: analyzing primary sources)
Includes bibliographical references and index.
Issued in print and electronic formats.
ISBN 978-0-7787-4814-4 (hardcover).--
ISBN 978-0-7787-4828-1 (softcover).--
ISBN 978-1-4271-2091-5 (HTML)

    1. United States--History--Civil War, 1861-1865--Juvenile
literature. 2. United States--History--Civil War,
1861-1865--Sources--Juvenile literature. I. Title.

E468.K67 2018   j973.7   C2017-907719-8
                                       C2017-907720-1

Library of Congress Cataloging-in-Publication Data

Names: Kopp, Megan, author.
Title: The Civil War / Megan Kopp.
Description: New York : Crabtree Publishing, 2018. |
    Series: Uncovering the past: analyzing primary sources |
    Includes bibliographical references and index.
Identifiers: LCCN 2017057932 (print) | LCCN 2017058310 (ebook) |
    ISBN 9781427120915 (Electronic) |
    ISBN 9780778748144 (hardcover : alk. paper) |
    ISBN 9780778748281 (pbk. : alk. paper)
Subjects: LCSH: United States--History--Civil War,
    1861-1865--Juvenile literature.
Classification: LCC E468 (ebook) | LCC E468 .K75 2018 (print) |
    DDC 973.7--dc23
LC record available at https://lccn.loc.gov/2017057932

Crabtree Publishing Company

www.crabtreebooks.com   1-800-387-7650

Printed in the U.S.A./022018/CG20171220

Published in Canada
Crabtree Publishing
616 Welland Ave.
St. Catharines, ON
L2M 5V6

Published in the United States
Crabtree Publishing
PMB 59051
350 Fifth Avenue, 59th Floor
New York, NY 10118

Published in the United Kingdom
Crabtree Publishing
Maritime House
Basin Road North, Hove
BN41 1WR

Published in Australia
Crabtree Publishing
3 Charles Street
Coburg North
VIC, 3058

UNCOVERING THE PAST

THE PAST COMES ALIVE

"A house divided against itself cannot stand."

President Abraham Lincoln in a speech to the
Republican State Convention in 1858

We study the past to try to understand people, places, and events. This history often allows us to interpret the present and make educated choices in the future. A **historian**'s role is to examine a vast array of sources of information to get a sense of a particular time and place. The tricky part is determining what sources are accurate, which ones are unfair, and which ones are completely false. Historians need to rely on critical thinking skills to build a clear picture of the past.

In the United States, the **Civil War** was a defining moment in history. It decided what type of nation the country would become. At the time—the early 1860s—the country was divided into **Union** and **Confederate** states. The war pitted family against family, neighbor against neighbor, state against state. Understanding this division is difficult today.

A variety of sources of information can help build a better sense of understanding. Historians studying the American Civil War use photographs, diaries, letters, **telegrams**, books, posters, political **cartoons,** and sketches to fill in the gaps in their knowledge and obtain a clearer picture of what happened and why.

The political cartoon on the opposite page is rich in detail. Uncle Sam wears a Union flag as a shirt. The woman wears a Confederate flag as an apron. One reason for this quarrel is **portrayed** by the **enslaved person** quietly trying to disappear in the background. Why do you think is smiling? Read on to get an insight.

A FAMILY QUARREL.

▲ This political cartoon was created sometime between 1861 and 1870 by a company with offices based in New York City and Washington, D.C. Which side of the war do you think this company supported? What leads you to believe this?

▲ A huge crowd of people—ordinary citizens, politicians, White House staff and their families—gather at President Abraham Lincoln's first **inauguration** at the U.S. Capitol, Washington, D.C., on March 4, 1861. At the time, photography was a new way of recording history. It turned out to be a major source of evidence of the Civil War.

EVIDENCE RECORD CARD

Lincoln inauguration photo by unknown photographer
LEVEL Primary source
MATERIAL Black-and-white photograph
LOCATION Washington, D.C.
DATE March 4, 1861
SOURCE Library of Congress

THE PATH TO WAR

The United States was showing signs of division long before the Civil War. Enslaved people helped fuel the **economy** of the country in its early years. By the early-1800s, the northern states, or North, had abolished slavery. The economy in the north was more industrialized. Factories used paid laborers. The opposite was true in the southern states. Slavery was legal and profitable in the South. There, 80 percent of the labor force was in agriculture. Southerners felt strongly that it was their right to decide whether to have slaves.

Rapid expansion in the west of the country brought unrest. There was an uneasy balance of power between free states and slave states. Did the newly formed territories have the right to adopt slavery? Abraham Lincoln won the presidential election in 1860. He promised to keep slavery out of the territories. Seven slave states formed the Confederate States of America. Civil war loomed.

PERSPECTIVES

These two unidentified soldiers are from the South. Why do you think it was it important for them to be photographed?

◀ Two soldiers, probably from North Carolina, in Confederate lieutenants' uniforms.

"We are not enemies, but friends. We must not be enemies. Though passion may have strained, it must not break our bonds of affection. The mystic chords of memory, stretching from every battlefield and patriot grave to every living heart and hearth-stone, all over this broad land, will yet swell the chorus of the Union, when again touched, as surely they will be, by the better angels of our nature."

President Abraham Lincoln in his inaugural address

▲ This stereo image from a prison in Alexandria, Virginia, for slaves waiting to be sold to a Union prison for military captives, illustrates the drastic changes war brought to the country.

It seemed like there would be no contest. Southern **secession** was viewed as illegal. The United States was recognized as a **legitimate** government. It could obtain loans and other favors if necessary. The population in the North was greater than that of the South, giving it a bigger military force and more workers for the many factories and industries that would produce materials needed for war. The North had a solid transportation system, including railroads.

The Union Navy was strong and its army was well-supplied and trained.

On the other hand, Southerners historically encouraged youth to sign up for military school or serve in the armed forces. Many southern soldiers and officers served in the U.S. Army. When it became a matter of Confederate States of America versus the United States, they chose to fight with the Confederate Army for their rights as states and their freedom as outlined in the **Constitution**.

DEFINITIONS

The Constitution is the guiding **document** for the United States of America. During the Civil War, the states in the north of the country were referred to as the Union. The Confederate States of America in the south were also known as the **Confederacy**. A confederacy is an alliance or group joined together to achieve a common goal. The South's secession was the act of leaving the Union and creating a separate government with its own guiding document. Several **border states** did not take sides in the American Civil War.

TYPES OF EVIDENCE

"My Very Dear Wife:

Indications are very strong that we shall move in a few days, perhaps to-morrow. Lest I should not be able to write you again, I feel impelled to write a few lines…"

Excerpt from Major Sullivan Ballou's last letter to his wife before losing his life in combat

Evidence is a body of facts or information that proves a belief or point. Historians are people who study evidence. They use **source material** as evidence of past events. Source materials are anything created during or about the time in history being studied. They include **artifacts**, recordings, books, photographs, paintings, maps, and more. Source materials can be found in libraries, **archives,** newspapers, museums, private collections, and on trusted Internet websites. Interviews of people who were involved or watched events are also sources.

The Civil War was a pivotal event in American history. Many sources recorded it. The war happened at a time when cameras were first being used. Newspapers sent photographers and **journalists** to record events. Participants on both sides of the battle wrote journals, diaries, and books about their experiences. Artists sketched and painted scenes from battlefields. Soldiers wrote letters home to their families.

Historians **analyze** and interpret these sources to learn about the beliefs and **culture** of the time of the Civil War. The military and political conflicts of the war had a major influence on people and **society** that continued to shape the nation long after the event was over. This knowledge can help us understand how we can prevent similar events in the future.

▼ This map shows Union and Confederate positions during the Battle of Fredericksburg, Virginia, on December 13, 1862.

Union army Cost in both Attacks 12,321. Killed wounded and missing.
Rebels Cost 5,309.

GENERAL WILCOX, C. S. A.

Official Plan by Topog Engineers of Kinney's Division 3rd Corps

E of FREDERICKSBURG Virginia - Shewing Union & Rebel Positions 13ᵈ Decr. 1862

at opening of Battle - 1.15 P.M. on Left of Union Line at HAMILTON'S CROSSING.

Union Forces 40,000 under Franklin   Rebel Forces under Jackson

PRIMARY SOURCES

There are two main types of source materials—**primary** and **secondary.** Primary sources are firsthand accounts by people who personally witnessed or took part in events at the time they occurred.

You create primary sources every day. When you complete a homework assignment, write in a journal or a blog, send an email, text your friends, or snap a picture at a football game, you are creating evidence of your life and time that could be used by future historians to understand what life is like today.

Primary sources include:

- Diaries and journals: Articles written down about daily life
- Newspapers: Printed reports on daily events in a certain area
- Blogs: Journals posted on the Internet
- Reports: Documents written for businesses or governments to show progress
- Photographs, paintings, and sketches: These are all visual records
- Lyrics: The words of a song
- Letters: **Correspondence** on paper between two people
- Artifacts: Objects found and collected at historical sites

An interesting primary source that developed in the Civil War was the **telegram.** Unlike diaries or books, these short messages were direct and left little to be interpreted. They provided immediate responses in the heat of battle and were not softened by time and fading memory. Abraham Lincoln kept in touch with his generals via telegrams. It was a new form of communication on the battlefield and unprecedented in its use as a war tool.

During the Civil War approximately 15,000 miles (24,140 km) of telegraph wire was strung for military purposes in the North. The telegram was a tool for sending and receiving information, much like today's press releases, social media posts, or cable newscasts.

Diaries, letters, and photographs from the Civil War provide unique insights into the lives and times of the soldiers and citizens involved—both Union and Confederate, North and South.

Primary sources such as these can be found in libraries, museums, state archives, and local and state historical societies. They can often be viewed online, too. Researchers also tap into town and county historians, town hall records, town planning offices, churches, and community groups.

"The camera is the eye of history."
Civil War photographer,
Mathew Brady

ANALYZE THIS

Decorated envelopes, like those on page 11, were designed to create emotion. What emotional response do you think they raised in the people who received them? How did the envelopes help promote support for the war?

SOLDIER'S LETTER.

EVIDENCE RECORD CARD

Stamped, addressed, Civil War propaganda envelope for a letter

LEVEL Primary source
MATERIAL Printed paper
LOCATION United States
DATE June 22, 1862
SOURCE Library of Congress

◄ This **patriotic** Civil War envelope shows Columbia with a shield and the U.S. flag as well as the White House in Washington, D.C.

PERSPECTIVES

How important do you think this primary source is and why? Do you recognize this format? Why or why not? How important do you think this message was at that point in the war? How might this type of message be sent today?

► Telegram from General William T. Sherman to President Abraham Lincoln on December 12, 1864.

By telegraph from Fort Monroe

Head-Quarters Military Division of the Mississippi,

In the Field _____ 186

Savannah, Dec 22 1864

To his Excellency,
President Lincoln,

I beg to present you as a Christmas Gift the City of Savannah. with one hundred and fifty (150) heavy guns and plenty of ammunition. as also about twenty five thousand (25000) bales of cotton

W. T. Sherman
Maj Genl.

33 Col

SECONDARY SOURCES

It is estimated that more than 65,000 books have been written about the Civil War. A few are primary sources. The vast majority are secondary sources. An **autobiography** written by a Civil War general is a primary source. U.S. Army General Ulysses S. Grant wrote a **memoir** shortly before his death. It, too, is a primary source, about battles of the war.

A biography written by another writer that is based on the life of Ulysses S. Grant would be a secondary source. Secondary sources use one or more primary sources as the basis for their interpretation of an event such as the Civil War.

The person who created the secondary source did not experience firsthand the content of what they are writing about. Other secondary sources include

EVIDENCE RECORD CARD

Harper's Weekly front page

LEVEL Primary source
MATERIAL Journal
LOCATION New York City
DATE September 5, 1863
SOURCE Library of Congress

"Human-nature will not change. In any future great national trial, compared with the men of this, we shall have as weak, and as strong; as silly and as wise; as bad and good. Let us, therefore, study the incidents of this, as philosophy to learn wisdom from, and none of them as wrongs to be revenged."

Abraham Lincoln

▲ The image on the cover of this journal shows Confederate raider John Mosby and his men destroying Union supply wagons.

magazine articles, history books, and documentaries.

When it comes to the written word, there are more books about the Civil War than any other event in American history. Historians, authors, and artists use primary source diaries, letters, government speeches, bills, laws, and newspaper articles to create their pieces about how the war unfolded.

Some of these books are historical fiction. Fiction is a story made up by the author. Quite often, the author will base their story on actual facts. For example, *The Red Badge of Courage* is a **historical novel** written by Stephen Crane in 1895. He was a journalist. He never fought in the war, but he did interview dozens of Civil War veterans. Crane came to understand that war was not always full of heroes and tales of extreme bravery. He learned that there were soldiers who felt fear and doubt. There were even some who were cowards, but they felt trapped and had no choice but to be in the war. Few people are likely to write stories admitting their own cowardice. Crane's fictional tale brings this less-than-perfect reality to life.

PERSPECTIVES

There are different versions of history. This painting—a secondary source—is the artist's impression of a battle scene. Do you think the painting glorifies the Union generals? Why or why not? What elements of the painting give you that impression?

▼ This painting, by Ole Peter Hansen Balling, shows Union Army leader Ulysses S. Grant (in the center) and his generals.

DIFFERENT INTERPRETATIONS

Secondary sources can be divided into different categories. Michael Shaara's novel of 1974, *The Killer Angels,* was a fictional book about the Civil War Battle of Gettysburg, with characters and events that reflect reality. Margaret Mitchell's *Gone with the Wind* was published nearly 40 years earlier in 1936. It was slanted more toward fiction rather than fact. *Gone with the Wind* was made into a movie in 1939. Movies are secondary sources, although they can range from fictional accounts to documentaries based on factual events.

Educational textbooks containing detailed information about the Civil War, modern-day diagrams that interpret battlefield maps, websites featuring songs of the Civil War, and current magazine or newspaper articles about Union and Confederate states are also good examples of secondary sources. They all interpret and evaluate primary sources of information.

Encyclopedias and online sources such as Wikipedia and nonprofessional websites are often compilations of multiple secondary sources. They are sometimes classed as **tertiary** sources.

▼ *Gone with the Wind* was an epic historical romance set during the Civil War and involving a slave-owning family.

While tertiary sources can be a good starting point to get a basic understanding of the topic, they are not reliable enough to stand on their own. They require additional research to get the true picture. Primary sources are always more reliable, and generally more accurate, than secondary and tertiary sources. But they are not always foolproof, as the next chapter of this book explains.

The best primary and secondary sources are usually those created closest in time to the historical event. Think about interviewing Ulysses S. Grant when he was in battle against Confederate troops in 1863. Now imagine interviewing him 20 years later when he was working on his memoir, sick with cancer, and in financial difficulty. Which interview do you think would provide the most detailed and accurate account of the impact of war?

▼ Harriet Beecher Stowe's novel of 1852, *Uncle Tom's Cabin*, focused on the need to end slavery. It influenced the views about the Union.

135,000 SETS, 270,000 VOLUMES SOLD.

UNCLE TOM'S CABIN

FOR SALE HERE.

AN EDITION FOR THE MILLION, COMPLETE IN 1 Vol., PRICE 37 1-2 CENTS.
"   "   IN GERMAN. IN 1 Vol., PRICE 50 CENTS.
"   "   IN 2 Vols., CLOTH, 6 PLATES, PRICE $1.50.
SUPERB ILLUSTRATED EDITION. IN 1 Vol., WITH 153 ENGRAVINGS,
PRICES FROM $2.50 TO $5.00.

The Greatest Book of the Age.

ANALYZE THIS

What do you think the bookseller meant by "The Greatest Book of the Age"? Which side of the slavery issue do you think the bookseller is on and why?

"Let no one entertain a thought of re-constructing the old Union. The time for re-construction has past. The people of the North have interposed between us and them a wall of fire and a river of blood, so that henceforth we must live as separate States both independent and free to follow its own system of government and civilization, or one subject to the other. We can never live together again as members of one family, associated under a common government."

Article in *Staunton Spectator* (Virginia), October 8, 1861

INTERPRETATION

"War Begun!
The Traitors Fire the First Gun!
Fort Sumter Attacked!"

Headline from *The Alleghanian* (Ebensburg, PA) on April 18, 1861

A source of information is created for a particular reason. Perhaps a person wants to record his or her experiences, thoughts, or feelings about an event. He or she might write a diary or blog entry. If a group of people want to show support for one side in a conflict, they might create posters and banners that make fun of the other side. Regardless of what the source is, it is important to question the content in order to better understand it. Who created the source? Why did they create it? What does this source prove, claim, show, or say? Questions provide **context**, or a sense of time and place. They allow us to figure out how society and culture shape people's views on events.

All sources have some form of **bias**. Bias is the **perspective** or opinions a person might or might not have for or against something. Questioning the source helps uncover potential biases. People who create primary and secondary sources often show bias by including some of their personal feelings or beliefs in the piece, accidently or deliberately.

Historians analyze source materials to determine if they are valid, useful, and accurate. A biased source tries to change someone's perspective on a topic. If a source is **credible**, it will be fact-based and unbiased. A few things that indicate a source is biased include omitted facts, positive or negative word choices, extreme language, emotion, and political or religious viewpoints. Because each and every source probably has some bias, historians use a wide range of evidence and information.

▼ This photo, called "Completely Silenced!" shows dead Confederate soldiers after the Battle of Antietam, one of the bloodiest battles of the war. There were an estimated 22,717 casualties, or inuries, including 3,654 dead.

ANALYZE THIS

Headline from the *Anderson Intelligencer* in Anderson Court House, South Carolina, on April 17, 1861, read: ***Fort Sumter Given Up!! Nobody Hurt on Our Side!!!*** Consider the initial headline at the top of the page opposite and compare it to the headline above. What is it in each that shows bias?

ANALYZING BIAS

Primary sources include images as well as the written word. Photography was an important primary source of evidence for the American Civil War. The war is considered to be the first major conflict to be extensively photographed. There is a photo by Alexander Gardner titled, "A Sharpshooter's Last Sleep, Gettysburg, July 1863." It has become one of the defining images of the Civil War. The gun lying beside the body is not actually a sharpshooter's rifle. The soldier was probably not a sniper. The image was biased—arranged to tell the story the photographer wanted to pass on.

Finding trustworthy sources involves critical thinking and careful questioning.

With evidence from the Civil War, a historian may first ask if the source is from the Union or Confederate side. What battles had just taken place and who won? Does the source show a soldier's, politician's, or citizen's view?

It is always a good idea to compare at least two or more different sources, if possible. Do the sources have similar facts and information? Do they have opposing or contradictory viewpoints? If they do, which one is more credible?

The artworks of a Civil War battle on these two pages are perfect examples of different perspectives. The mostly

▼ Alexander Gardner's controversial image of a dead Confederate sharpshooter.

nighttime battle of Chickamauga was fought in the forests of Georgia near the border of Tennessee. Chickamauga Creek was deep, tree-lined, and bordered by rocky banks. Most of the areas where armies battled were in thickets. There were no clear sight lines. The armies had to constantly shift positions as they ran into one another unexpectedly. Knowing these details, which image is the most accurate?

Which piece of art do you think was created on the sidelines of the battlefield and which one do you think was prepared in the artist's studio? Would you be surprised to learn that the color illustration was created some 27 years after the battle took place? Does it show the Union or the Confederate forces winning the battle? Do you think it is biased or very realistic?

◄ A line of Confederate soldiers advances through forest toward Union troops at the Battle of Chickamauga, Georgia, as drawn by Alfred R. Waud in 1863.

▼ A color print of 1890 of the same battle.

"I am nothing, but truth is everything."

Abraham Lincoln, 1860

THE CIVIL WAR

"No Person held to Service or Labour in one State, under the Laws thereof, escaping into another, shall, in Consequence of any Law or Regulation therein, be discharged from such Service or Labour, but shall be delivered up, on Claim of the Party to whom such Service or Labour may be due."

The Fugitive Slave Clause in the original Constitution

The journey toward war was fueled by political actions and conflicting beliefs about slavery. In an effort to maintain peace between states, the Missouri **Compromise** of 1820 was passed to allow Maine to enter the Union as a free state, Missouri as a slave state, and declare any other territory north of Missouri's southern border free from slavery.

The Compromise of 1850 allowed California to join the Union as a free state. This upset the balance in **Congress,** making 16 free states and only 15 slave states. It also created the Fugitive Slave Act, taking control of returning runaway slaves from state to **federal** level. In 1854, the land west of Missouri was divided into a free and a slave territory. The Kansas–Nebraska Act allowed settlers in the new territories to decide if slavery would be legal there.

There had long been a moral opposition to slavery in the United States. Abolitionists wanted to end slavery, period. Other people opposed the spread of slavery into new territory. John Brown was an abolitionist who believed slavery would only end with a violent overthrow of the slavery system. In October 1859, he and 21 supporters seized a government **arsenal** at Harpers Ferry. They held it for two days before being captured. In a final attempt to avoid civil war, the Crittenden Compromise was proposed in 1860. It suggested an east–west line across the country, with freedom above and slavery below. Congress did not pass the proposal.

▼ In this 1859 painting, John Brown is led away from Harpers Ferry, West Virginia. Although he was executed as a traitor, he was also a hero to many.

PERSPECTIVES

This painting is full of tragedy and despair. Who are the people holding rifles? Why are the slave mother and child in the picture? What is the artist's message?

SECESSION AND SLAVE OWNERSHIP

On November 6, 1860, Abraham Lincoln was elected president of the United States. Just over a month later, South Carolina became the first state to leave the Union. In January 1861, the southern states of Mississippi, Florida, Alabama, Georgia, and Louisiana **seceded**. Texas followed in February. Together they created the Confederate Constitution with an emphasis on self-government. Jefferson Davis was named temporary president of the Confederacy until elections could be held. Richmond, Virginia, became the Confederate capital, or main city.

Lincoln was inaugurated as president of the United States in March 1861. Five weeks later, Confederate warships fired on Fort Sumter. The Union fought back. The Civil War had begun.

The state of Virginia had close ties with the North and the South, but on April 17 it seceded. Arkansas, North Carolina, and Tennessee would follow. Most southern slave owners were farmers and plantation owners. They believed that states' rights included the right to keep humans as property. Slavery was accepted as odd and unusual, but it was tied to the region's economy and the wealth and privilege of Southern elites. It was even called the "peculiar institution."

Southerners also felt they had the right to secede because they had voted to join the United States and the

PERSPECTIVES

This image and the newspaper opposite are two very different pieces of evidence for the start of the war. Which one do you feel has greater impact? Why? Are these primary or secondary sources?

▼ This watercolor painting of Fort Sumter under siege may have been drawn by an eyewitness. The fort, in South Carolina, had been occupied by Union forces opposed to the state's secession.

Constitution did not clearly say that they could not vote to leave. In his first inaugural address, Jefferson Davis stated, "Our present condition, achieved in a manner unprecedented in the history of nations, illustrates the American idea that governments rest upon the consent of the governed, and that it is the right of the people to alter or abolish governments whenever they become destructive of the ends for which they were established."

President Lincoln and his administration refused to recognize this idea. In his first inaugural address, Abraham Lincoln stated, "I hold that, in contemplation of universal law, and of the Constitution, the union of these States is perpetual. . . . It follows. . . .that no State, upon its own mere motion, can lawfully get out of the Union. . ." In a special session message to Congress on July 4, 1861, Lincoln added, "The States have their status in the Union, and they have no other legal status. If they break from this they can only do so against law and by **revolution.**"

▼ The front page of *The New York Times* on the second day of the war—April 13, 1861.

"*The time for compromise has now passed, and the South is determined to maintain her position, and make all who oppose her smell Southern powder and feel Southern steel.*"

Jefferson Davis, inaugural speech, February 16, 1861

BATTLE LINES ARE DRAWN

In 1861, the armies were equal in size. By 1863, the Union Army outnumbered the Confederate Army two to one. How did this come about? Enforced military service. It wasn't the North who started the first **draft** in American history; it was the Confederacy. However, there were about 22 million people living in the North and only some nine million in the South (including four million slaves) so the Union Army grew faster.

Regardless of size, both sides had big victories and major losses. On July 21, 1861, the first major battle erupted at Manassas, Virginia. The First Battle of Bull Run lasted only one day, but it was the testing ground for both armies. It was here that General "Stonewall" Jackson earned his nickname for standing "like a wall" in the face of Union fire.

Residents from Washington, D.C., arrived in carriages to watch the show, which quickly turned into a horrible

▲ President Lincoln (center, with tall hat) and General McClellan (fourth from right) at the Union Army of Potomac headquarters just before the Battle of Antietam on September 17, 1862.

"No tongue can tell, no mind conceive, no pen portray the horrible sights I witnessed."
Soldier at the Battle of Antietam

reality. With about 4,500 casualties, it was the bloodiest battle in U.S. history up to that time. Virginia would become the battleground for more conflicts than any other state due to its proximity to the capital cities of Washington, D.C., and Richmond, Virginia.

The Battle of Antietam near Sharpsburg, Maryland, was another showstopper. It was the first major battle in the North. Confederate General Robert E. Lee and Union General George McClellan faced off in bloody **rout** that saw the greatest number of casualties of any single-day battle of the Civil War. McClellan had numbers on his side, but he was unable to defeat Lee's army. The result was a draw but the Union claimed victory. After Antietam, Lincoln relieved McClelland of supreme command. He was an excellent organizer, but he was reluctant to fight.

Shortly after Antietam, President Lincoln issued the **Emancipation Proclamation**. On September 22, 1862, he declared that effective from January 1, 1863, all slaves in "enemy territory" were free. At the same time, African Americans were finally allowed to enlist and fight on behalf of the Union.

PERSPECTIVES

Female nurses tended wounded soldiers of the Civil War, near battlefields and in hospitals. Compare this illustration with the primary source images of battlefields on pages 16–17 and 28–29.

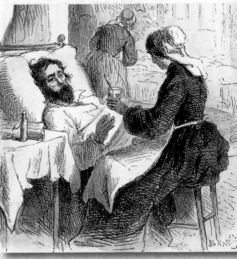

▲ The Civil War was not a show of power and dominance but suffering.

◄ Photographers faced the horror of war as a job. A relatively new technology, photography showed the world what war was really like for the first time.

EVIDENCE RECORD CARD

Sailors relaxing on the deck of the U.S.S. *Monitor*

LEVEL Primary source
MATERIAL Photograph
PHOTOGRAPHER J. Gibson
LOCATION James River, VA
DATE July 9, 1862
SOURCE Library of Congress

DIVIDE AND CONQUER

Fort Sumter was located on an island in the Charleston Harbor, South Carolina. When it was attacked by Confederate ships, the Union stronghold was accessible only by boat. Control of waterways quickly became a key to success in the war.

In an effort to stall the Confederate economy and cut off international support, President Lincoln issued **blockades**. Although not watertight, the blockades slowed down the export of cotton and imports of supplies for war. There were questions in international law about the legality of the blockades, but the U.S government successfully convinced foreign governments that it was a legitimate war tool. By July 1862, the Union Navy had blockades on all of the major southern ports.

◀ Union sailors take time to relax aboard the deck of the U.S.S. *Monitor*.

▼ Ironclad ships were a new invention that came out of the American Civil War.

THE FIRST FIGHT BETWEEN IRON CLAD SHIPS OF WAR.
TERRIFIC COMBAT BETWEEN THE "MONITOR" 2 GUNS & "MERRIMAC" 10 GUNS.
IN HAMPTON ROADS, MARCH 9TH 1862.
In which the little "Monitor" whipped the "Merrimac" and the whole "School" of Rebel Steamers.

As the war progressed, taking control of waterways took a turn. In an effort to undermine the Union Navy's strength, Confederate engineers turned an old Union ship, the U.S.S. *Merrimac,* into an iron-sided vessel. It was renamed the C.S.S. *Virginia.* In March of 1862, the *Virginia* sank two Union warships off Norfolk, Virginia. The Union Navy sent their "ironclad," the U.S.S. *Monitor,* to take on the Virginia. It was a draw, but not before the shape of war was changed forever.

In 1863, the Union Army focused on regaining control of the Mississippi River. Vicksburg was a fortified city on the waterway. General Ulysses S. Grant led the Vicksburg **Campaign** and, after six weeks of siege, the Confederates gave up the city. Port Hudson, Louisiana, followed next. The entire Mississippi was now under Union control. The Confederacy was split in two.

Another blow came when Union General William Tecumseh Sherman began his infamous "March to the Sea." He led his army into Georgia and South Carolina, destroying everything that could possibly help the Confederate Army. Nothing was spared as factories, bridges, railroads, and even public buildings were razed.

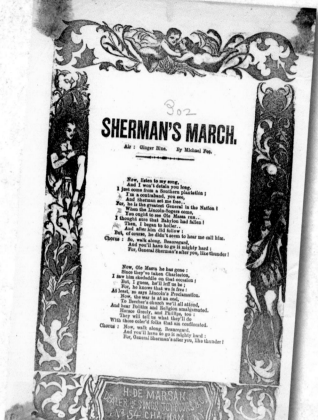

▶ American Civil War **broadsides**, such as this one, are primary sources as they were created during the war.

"Damn the torpedoes!"
Rear Admiral David G. Farragut's infamous phrase called out during the Battle of Mobile Bay as his Union ship surged past Confederate forces.

ANALYZE THIS

This broadside threatens Confederate troops by glorifying Union generals, especially Major General William T. Sherman. How effective do you think this would be in affecting the morale of soldiers on the Confederate side? What effect might it have on Union soldiers?

GETTYSBURG BATTLE AND ADDRESS

At the start of the Gettysburg Campaign of June 3 to July 14, 1863, Union General Joseph Hooker put up a manned air balloon to view the enemy position. He saw the Confederates moving north and thought it was an opportunity to move against their capital. Lincoln used the telegraph system to set him straight.

"If left to me, I would not go South of the Rappahannock, upon Lee's moving North of it. . . . I think Lee's army, and not Richmond, is your true objective point."

With every major battle occurring on southern soil, Confederate General Lee hoped to take the fight into the North. The Battle of Gettysburg would dash that hope. The three-day battle started on July 1, 1863. The Confederate forces were finally forced to retreat back to the southern side of the Potomac River, but not before some 50,000 lives were lost.

On November 19, 1863, President Lincoln delivered the Gettysburg Address at the dedication of the Soldiers' National Cemetery at Gettysburg, Pennsylvania. He was not the main speaker that day. The first speech given was two hours long. Lincoln's was a short, two-minute, 272-word

▼ A primary source photograph of dead horses on the battlefield at Gettysburg. The house in the photo acted as headquarters of Union General Daniel Edgar Sickles.

"Let us give these southern fellows all the fighting they want and when they are tired we can tell them we are just warming to the work."

William T. Sherman to Ulysses S. Grant in 1864

PERSPECTIVES

What do you see first when you look at this photo? How do you think Union and Confederate soldiers felt looking at this scene? What might a news reporter say?

speech. Still, it became one of the most recognizable speeches in U.S. history.

"Four score and seven years ago our fathers brought forth on this continent a new nation, conceived in liberty, and dedicated to the proposition that all men are created equal…"

For three years, from 1862 to 1865, Confederate General Robert E. Lee's Army of North Virginia kept fighting and dodging invasions and attacks by the Union's Army of the Potomac. President Lincoln finally found the key he needed to turn the tide when Ulysses S. Grant became the general of all chiefs in 1864.

PERSPECTIVES

This is the only picture of the Gettysburg Address with Abraham Lincoln. Can you pick him out of this photograph? How can you distinguish the different people in the crowd? How might this image be different with today's photographic equipment?

▶ The crowd gathers to hear Lincoln's Gettysburg Address.

COUNTING THE LOSSES

In 1864, General Grant started the Overland Campaign against Lee. Union forces had the manpower and materials even though Lee's Army of Northern Virginia had the home advantage. The Army of the Potomac was twice the size of the Confederate Army. Grant's goal was simple—no-holds-barred destruction of the rebel forces.

After Gettysburg, Lee's Army of Northern Virginia entrenched along the Rapidan River. It was here the two generals and their forces would face off in the Battles of the Wilderness, Spotsylvania Court House, North Anna River, Totopotomoy Creek, and Cold Harbor. After 40 days of maneuvers and combat, Grant lost about 55,000 men. Lee saw losses tallying approximately 33,000.

Grant hoped to take Petersburg, south of the Confederate capital, starting in June of 1864, but the attempt failed. The result was a 10-month siege. Thousands more lives were lost on both sides.

On March 25, 1865, General Lee attacked General Grant's forces near Petersburg, just south of the Confederate capital of Richmond, Virginia. His army was defeated, but

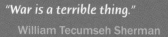

"War is a terrible thing."
William Tecumseh Sherman

▲ This color image of the burning of Richmond, Virginia, highlights the destruction of the city as well as military losses.

he struck again on April 1. The next day, the Confederate forces under Lee's command evacuated Richmond and moved west. Jefferson Davis ordered Confederate government officials to leave. The destruction of the war was evident in ravaged buildings and uncontained fires. Much of the destruction was captured by photographer Alexander Gardner.

On April 7, Lee and his troops were surrounded. General Grant called on Lee to surrender. Both sides knew that this was the end. Two days later the two generals met in Appomattox Court House and agree on terms of the Confederate surrender. Lee's men were sent home on **parole**. Soldiers were allowed to keep their horses and officers to keep their sidearms, but everything else was surrendered. The battle— and the Civil War—was almost over. Confederate President Jefferson Davis was captured in Georgia on May 10.

The tally for the war is horrendous. More than 330,000 Union soldiers and 250,000 Confederate soldiers were killed in battle or died from disease. About 50,000 civilians were killed. Thousands of soldiers as well as African American freedmen were buried at Arlington National Cemetery in Virginia.

▼ Returned Union prisoners of war exchange their rags for new clothing after they board the *Flag of Truce* ship.

PERSPECTIVES

What story do you think the artist was trying to convey in this image? Do you think this image is a primary or secondary source? Why?

AT HOME AND ABROAD

"Let us cross over the river, and rest under the shade of the trees."

"Stonewall" Jackson's last words

The Civil War affected all of the nation. On April 14, 1865, President Lincoln was assassinated by John Wilkes Booth. Lincoln died the next day. Booth escaped to Virginia after the shooting but was shot and killed by a Union soldier 11 days later. The final battle of the Civil War happened less than a month later, on May 13, at Palmito Ranch, Texas.

Even though California and Oregon were across the country from most of the Civil War action, they still had a role to play. In September 1861, a senator from Oregon was sent to Philadelphia to fund and command the California Brigade. The brigade joined the fight against the Confederacy. Other Eastern-born Californians also joined forces and headed east to join the fight. The California Column, a group of 5,000 Union volunteers, marched 900 miles (1,448 km) to Texas in order to keep Confederate soldiers out of Arizona Territory and remove them from New Mexico. This was key to keeping the South from gaining support and strength in the west.

Back in California, the state's gold resources were important for the Union. The Confederacy could have benefited from the gold and access to ports unaffected by the Union blockade. A small number of Southerners who moved to the state during the 1848–1857 gold rush were vocal about having Southern California secede from the Union. In 1864, Confederate Captain Rufus Ingram began recruiting Southern Californians to join him in robbing stagecoaches. The money they took was used to fund the Confederate cause. The state definitely felt the impact of the war, and it took many years for divisions to heal.

▶ This **lithograph** is a secondary source showing the artist's interpretation of the assassination of Abraham Lincoln by John Wilkes Booth.

► Theater tickets to Ford's Theatre on the night of the attack are primary sources.

PERSPECTIVES

How do you think the artist knew that there were four people plus Booth in the president's theatre box, and that Booth had a gun and a dagger? What primary sources might the artist have used to gather the details to create this art? Search trusted sources on the Internet to find images of artifacts that exist from the event.

DIFFERENT VIEWS

INTERNATIONAL INFLUENCES

European nations watched the American Civil War carefully. Most nations strove to remain neutral through the conflict. Southern cotton was sold to France and **Britain**. The Confederacy hoped that these countries would come to their defense in order to protect this resource. France stated a hands-off position. Britain had a stockpile of enough cotton to tide them over until they could find new markets, but it wasn't until the Emancipation Proclamation was issued that its head of

▼ In the mid-1800s, most of the world's cotton was produced within the Confederate states with the use of slaves.

▶ After the war, the U.S. government claimed compensation was due from Britain because of the damage to Union ships done by the *Alabama*, a ship built in Britain for the Confederacy.

No. 2.   COTTON IS KING!

Old England is mighty; Old England is free;
She boasts that she ruleth the waves of the sea;
(But between you and I, that's all fiddle-de-dee;)
She cannot, O Cotton! she cannot rule thee.
Lo! Manchester's lordling thy greatness shall own,
And yield more to thee than he would to the Throne;
For before thee shall bend his fat marrow-bone,
And deaf be his ear to the live chattel's groan.

Entered according to Act of Congress, in the year 1861, by STIMSON & Co., in the Clerk's Office of the United States for the Southern District of New-York.

ANALYZE THIS

Cartoon images are often used to get across very serious messages. The relationship between Britain and the United States during the Civil War was tenuous. When the United States gained the upper hand, the results were ideal for cartoons, as is the case with President Lincoln offering "Humble Pie" to the British.

"And we do hereby strictly charge and command all our loving subjects to observe a strict neutrality in and during the aforesaid hostilities, and to abstain from violating or contravening either the laws and statutes of the realm in this behalf or the law of nations in relation thereto, as they will answer to the contrary at their peril."

Queen Victoria's Royal Proclamation regarding the American Civil War

state, Queen Victoria, reconfirmed its policy of neutrality.

After the Confederate states seceded from the United States, the Union government issued a worldwide warning against foreign involvement. A few British citizens and businesses quietly aided the Confederate cause. Most of the Confederate warships were built in Liverpool, England.

Britain came close to being actively involved during the war during the Trent Affair. The *Trent* was a British ship. Jefferson Davis snuck two commissioners representing Confederate interests in France and England through the Union blockade. When they reached a neutral port in

Cuba, they boarded the *Trent*. A Federal warship discovered their whereabouts, boarded the ship, and took the commissioners into custody.

There was an immediate outcry by Britain about the legality of this action. About 11,000 troops were sent to Canada. The British fleet was put on standby. A strongly worded notice was sent to the United States demanding surrender of the prisoners and an apology. President Lincoln **conceded** and the Trent Affair was set aside.

Although Canada was still under control of Britain during the Civil War, thousands of Canadians served in the Union Army. Southern commissioners and escaped prisoners of war traveled to Canada as well. Canadian courts recognized them as military **belligerents** who were simply following orders as opposed to rebels, and they refused to send the prisoners of war back to the United States.

▼ When the Confederacy formed its own government, it was on its own and produced its own monetary system. These are Confederate banknotes.

A VARIETY OF INTERPRETATIONS

One of the most infamous historical sources associated with the pre-Civil War era is Harriet Beecher Stowe's novel, *Uncle Tom's Cabin*. It was inspired by true slave stories, primarily *The Life of Josiah Henson, Formerly a Slave, Now an Inhabitant of Canada, as Narrated by Himself*. Stowe's main goal in writing this book was to convince people of the need to end slavery. She lived for a while in a slave state and interviewed escaped slaves as well as writer and abolitionist leader Frederick Douglass. *Uncle Tom's Cabin* was the first American novel to sell more than a million copies. Analyzing the book, while acknowledging the author's biases, helps us understand why the Civil War happened.

ANALYZE THIS

What's in a name? Based on the titles of these two books dealing with the Civil War, what types of historical sources do you think they are? What might you use the books for in your research about the war, and why: *The Mostly True Adventures of Homer P. Figg*, a 2009 children's book by W.R. Philbrick, and Russell Freedman's 1987 book, *Lincoln: A Photobiography*.

◀ A poster for a 1899 play based on of H.B. Stowe's novel. Many of the early play versions of Uncle Tom's Cabin dealt in offensive stereotypes that distorted the book's meaning and intent.

"But how nice it would be to know that some good Yankee woman—And there must be SOME good Yankee women. I don't care what people say, they can't all be bad! How nice it would be to know that they pulled weeds off our men's graves and brought flowers to them, even if they were enemies."

Melanie in Margaret Mitchell's *Gone with the Wind*

The Civil War itself was the topic of tens of thousands of books. There were diaries made into books such as Mary Chesnut's *A Diary from Dixie*. Mary Chesnut was married to a U.S. senator from South Carolina. He resigned to work with the Confederacy. Mary recorded her personal views and observations. While a diary itself is a primary source, a book penned after the fact sometimes becomes a secondary source. The author might **embellish** events later as time and distance alters memories.

While there was not much published about African American soldiers during or soon after the war, historians and authors are now filling in the gaps. John David Smith edited a 2003 book entitled *Black Soldiers in Blue*. Fourteen original essays tell the stories of African American soldiers who fought for the Union cause. These essays delve into the military, political, and social significance of African American soldiers' armed service, including an essay about these veterans postwar in North Carolina. *The United States Colored Troops: The History and Legacy of the Black Soldiers Who Fought in the American Civil War* includes accounts of the battles written by black soldiers. It follows the development and impact of African American regiments on the second half of the war.

MARY CHESNUT
A Diary from Dixie

The Civil War's most celebrated journal, written during the conflict by the wife of Confederate General James Chesnut, Jr.

PERSONAL MEMOIRS OF U. S. GRANT

▶ *A Diary from Dixie* is still in print today.

▶ Ulysses S. Grant would go on from being a Union general to becoming the 18th President of the United States.

HISTORY REPEATED

"Lay aside all rancor, all bitter sectional feeling, and to make your places in the ranks of those who will bring about a consummation devoutly to be wished—a reunited country."

Jefferson Davis, 1888

Officially, by the summer of 1866 the American Civil War was over. However, states still struggled against federal policies, and racism continued to be a dividing issue. Similar modern struggles have gone on, and continue to go on, around the world. Many stem from conflicting political beliefs. The American Civil War did as well, although the issue of slavery— the "peculiar institution"—made it unusual.

The Spanish Civil War from 1936 to 1939 started as a military revolt against the government. When the military failed to gain control of the entire country in its first attempt, civil war erupted. The Nationalists, as the rebellious military forces were called, were mostly **fascists** supporting wealthy landowners. The Nationalists received support, including money, from Italy and Germany. The Republicans were **socialists** supporting workers and the educated middle-class. They received aid from the **Soviet Union** and volunteers from Europe and the North America. The 2,800 American volunteers were called the Abraham Lincoln Brigade.

The Nationalists leaned toward dictatorship and the denial of human rights. They won the war. When dictator Francisco Franco took control of the country, he stayed in power for 36 years. The Spanish Civil War lasted just under three years. About 600,000 people lost their lives in direct battle. Both the American and Spanish Civil Wars were battles against world views of how a country should be governed and run, and they came at a great cost.

▼ A group of Republican militia fighters during the start of the Spanish Civil War in 1936. Photography was now one of the most important historical sources and powerful forms of propaganda. In Spain, both sides of the conflict used it to attract supporters and frighten the opposition.

PERSPECTIVES

How does this fighting force differ from the Union and Confederate armies of the American Civil War? Do you think it would be as well trained and effective in war? Why or why not? Does the photo look real or posed?

CLOSING BORDERS AND OLD DIVISIONS

Following the Civil War, the United States entered a period of rebuilding known as the Reconstruction. For the next 12 years, the country worked to reunite. People disagreed on how to bring the seceding states back into the Union and grant full citizenship to formerly enslaved people. All civil wars are involve fights over power and rights and winners and losers. Healing the wounds of war can take decades or even centuries. In the United States today, one legacy of the war may be continued divided opinion on the war's causes and how to commemorate it.

There has been a lot of reflection on how history is reproduced, whose stories are told and whose stories are missing. American Civil War stories are often told as public history in the form of monuments and statues. Some people want monuments that represent the Confederacy removed from public places and placed in museums where they can be shown as artefacts of history.

There are more than 700 Confederate statues on public property and spaces in 31 states, including Washington, D.C. Some of these were erected in the 1950s and 1960s—100 years after the war ended. Strong reaction to their removal has raised the level of tension in many places. There are few memorials commemorating the close to 200,000 African Americans who served in the U.S. Army during the Civil War or the approximately 40,000 who lost their lives in the battles. Those memorials that do exist were put up in the last 10 years or so. The legacy of the Civil War continues to change and evolve with time.

"Although a soldier by profession, I have never felt any sort of fondness for war, and I have never advocated it, except as a means of peace."

Ulysses S. Grant, in a speech given in London, England, in 1877

A crowd surrounds a statue of Confederate General Gustave Toutant Beauregard in New Orleans. It was one of four Confederate monuments removed throughout the city in 2017. The 102-year-old statue is now in storage.

Demonstrators call for the Confederate flag to remain on the State House grounds on June 27, 2015, in Columbia, South Carolina.

ANALYZE THIS

Look at these two photos. What messages do they give you? What do they tell you about American society at the time they were taken? Who do you think took the photos? Are there any obvious biases? If so, what are they? How closely do they relate to your understanding of the issues of the Civil War? What are your opinions about war? Was it necessary? What did it achieve, if anything?

TIMELINE

1820 The Missouri Compromise

1850 The Compromise of 1850

1854 Kansas–Nebraska Act

November 6, 1860 Abraham Lincoln elected 16th President of the United States

January 1861 Mississippi, Florida, Georgia, Alabama, and Louisiana secede from the Union

April 12, 1861 First shots fired at Fort Sumter, starting the Civil War

April 22, 1861 Robert E. Lee accepts command of Virginia forces

July 21, 1861 First major battle at Manassas (Bull Run), Virginia

April 16, 1862 Slavery abolished in District of Columbia

August 28, 1862 Battle of Second Manassas begins; ends with a Confederate victory

1862 President Lincoln issues his Emancipation Proclamation; effective from January 1, 1863

March 3, 1863 Lincoln signs the Conscription Act, creating the first military draft in the United States

May, 1863 Confederate General T. J. "Stonewall" Jackson accidentally shot by his own men and dies

July 1, 1863 Battle of Gettysburg, Pennsylvania begins

November 19, 1863 President Lincoln delivers the Gettysburg Address

---

1820

1861

1862

1863

1852 *Uncle Tom's Cabin* published

1859 John Brown raids Harpers Ferry, Virginia

December 20, 1860 South Carolina secedes from the Union

February 1, 1861 Texas secedes from the Union

February 9, 1861 Jefferson Davis elected Confederate President

April 19, 1861 President Lincoln declares a blockade of Southern ports

1861 Virginia, Arkansas, North Carolina, and Tennessee secede

March 9, 1862 Battle of the USS *Monitor* and the *Virginia*

May 5, 1862 Battle of Williamsburg, Virginia

September 17, 1862 Battle of Antietam, Maryland, begins

1863 Lincoln authorizes Treasury to print $100,000,000 in new notes to pay soldiers

April 30, 1863 Battle of Chancellorsville begins near Fredericksburg, Virginia

May 18, 1863 First attack on Vicksburg, Mississippi, begins; Confederates surrender on July 4

September 19, 1863 Battle of Chickamauga, Georgia, begins

1864 Abraham Lincoln nominated for 2nd term as U.S. president

May 7, 1864 Sherman begins his Atlanta campaign

July 22, 1864 Battle of Atlanta, Georgia, begins

November 8, 1864 Abraham Lincoln re-elected as U.S. President

November 30, 1864 Sherman leaves Atlanta on his March to the Sea

December 15, 1864 Battle of Nashville, Tennessee, begins

February 5, 1865 Battle of Hatcher's Run, Virginia, begins

1865 Jefferson Davis signs law allowing African American men to serve in Confederate Army

April 9, 1865 General Lee surrenders to General Grant

December 6, 1865 13th Amendment becomes part of the Constitution

1864

1865

1866

July 20, 1864 Battle of Peachtree Creek, Georgia, begins

August 5, 1864 Battle of Mobile, Alabama, begins

November 30, 1864 Battle of Franklin, Tennessee,

January 31, 1865 13th Amendment abolishing slavery is passed

March 6, 1865 Battle of Natural Bridge, Florida

April 2, 1865 Confederate government evacuates Richmond, Virginia

April 15, 1865 Abraham Lincoln dies after being shot the eveing before

August 20, 1866 President Johnson announces official end of the war

Map of the United States showing Union, Confederate, and nonaligned states

BIBLIOGRAPHY

QUOTATIONS AND EXCERPTS

P. 4 Lincoln, Abraham. *The Library of Congress Civil War Desk Reference*, 2009, p. 116.

P. 6 Lincoln, Abraham. https://www.civilwar.org/learn/primary-sources/lincolns-first-inaugural-address

P. 8 Ballou, Sullivan. https://www.civilwar.org/learn/primary-sources/sullivan-ballou-letter

P. 10 Brady, Mathew. http://ushistoryscene.com/article/civil-war-photography/

P. 12 Lincoln, Abraham. November 10, 1864: In Response to a Serenade. https://www.nps.gov/liho/learn/historyculture/1864election.htm

P. 15 Article in *Staunton Spectator* (Virginia), October 8, 1861. http://valley.lib.virginia.edu/news/ss1861/va.au.ss.1861.10.08.xml#01

P. 19 Lincoln, Abraham. http://www.bartleby.com/348/authors/328.html

P. 20 Fugitive Slave Clause in the original Constitution. http://www.ucs.louisiana.edu/~ras2777/amgov/secession.html

P. 23 Davis, Jefferson. https://civilwartalk.com/threads/davis-jefferson.8500/

P. 24 Unknown. https://www.nlm.nih.gov/exhibition/lifeandlimb/education.html

P. 27 Farragut, David G. http://www.essentialcivilwarcurriculum.com/the-battle-of-mobile-bay.html

P. 28 Sherman, William T. William T. Sherman to Ulysses S. Grant, August 7, 1864 in United States War Department, *The War of the Rebellion: A Compilation of the Official Records of the Union and Confederate Armies*, Series I, volume 38, part 5, p. 408.

P. 30 Sherman, William T. https://civilwartalk.com/threads/william-t-sherman-warns-the-south.95202/

P. 32 Jackson, Thomas J. http://www.civilwarprofiles.com/did-stonewall-jackson-cross-or-pass-over-the-river-2/

P. 34 http://archive.spectator.co.uk/article/18th-may-1861/9/the-neutrality-proclamation

P. 36 https://ebooks.adelaide.edu.au/m/mitchell/margaret/gone/chapter41.html

P. 38 Davis, Jefferson. https://civilwartalk.com/threads/a-speech-from-jefferson-davis-in-1888.13444/

P. 40 Ulysses S. Grant. *In The Personal Memoirs of Julia Dent (Mrs. Ulysses S. Grant)*. New York, Putnam, 1975. page 205.

TO FIND OUT MORE

Alberti, Enigma. *Spy on History: Mary Bowser and the Civil War Spy Ring*. Workman, 2016.

Bearce, Stephanie. *Top Secret Files: The Civil War: Spies, Secret Mission and Hidden Facts from the Civil War*. Prufrock, 2014.

DK. *DK Eyewitness Books: Civil War*. DK Children, 2015.

Freedman, Russell and Robert Petkoff. *Lincoln: A Photobiography* (audiobook). Findaway World, 2013.

Isaacs, Sally Senzell. *All About America: The Civil War*. Kingfisher, 2011.

Nardo, Don. *Civil War Witness: Mathew Brady's Photos Reveal the Horrors of War*. Compass Point, 2013.

O'Connor, Jim. *What Was the Battle of Gettysburg?* Grosset & Dunlop, 2013.

Philbrick, Rodman. *The Mostly True Adventures of Homer P. Figg*. Blue Sky Press, 2009.

Putnam, Jeff. *A Nation Divided: Causes of the Civil War*. Crabtree, 2011.

INTERNET GUIDELINES

Finding good source material on the Internet can sometimes be a challenge. When analyzing how reliable the information is, consider these points:

- Who is the author of the page? Is it an expert in the field or a person who experienced the event?
- Is the site well known and up to date? A page that has not been updated for several years probably has out-of-date information.
- Can you verify the facts with another site? Always double-check information.

- Have you checked all possible sites? Don't just look on the first page a search engine provides. Remember to try government sites and research papers.
- Have you recorded website addresses and names? Keep this data so you can backtrack and verify the information you want to use.

WEBSITES:

Library of Congress Archives:
Solving a Civil War Photograph Mystery.
http://www.loc.gov/pictures/collection/cwp/mystery.html

The Valley of the Shadow:
Two Communities in the American Civil War.
http://valley.lib.virginia.edu

The Civil War Trust:
All about battlefields and their preservation.
https://www.civilwar.org

The American Civil War Museum:
A museum to visit in Richmond, Virginia, and an online resource.
https://acwm.org/

American Civil War History:
Facts, figures, photographs and videos about all aspects of the war.
http://www.history.com/topics/american-civil-war/american-civil-war-history

The Underground Railroad:
African American history related to slavery and the Underground Railroad.
https://www.nps.gov/nr/Travel/underground/

GLOSSARY

abolitionist Someone who worked to abolish slavery before the Civil War

analyze To examine closely

archive A place where historical documents are kept, or a group of documents themselves

arsenal A collection of weapons and military equipment stored by a country, person, or group

artifacts Objects made by people such as clothes, pottery, weapons, and coins

autobiography A book about a person's life written by that same person

belligerents Nations or people engaged in war or conflict, as recognized by international law

bias Prejudice in favor of or against one thing, person, or group compared with another

blockade An act or means of sealing off a place to prevent goods or people from entering or exiting

border states In the United States, slave states that did not leave the Union, such as Delaware, Kentucky, and Maryland

Britain A nation comprising England, Northern Ireland, Scotland, and Wales

broadsides A large sheet of paper printed on only one side

campaign A series of military operations intended to achieve a particular goal

cartoons Semi-realistic illustrations using caricatures

civil war A war between groups of people within a country

compromise Settlement of a dispute that is reached by each side making concessions

conceded To allow an opponent to win; to give up

confederacy An alliance of states or groups of people

Confederate The southern states that left the United States during the Civil War

Congress The legislative branch of government, including the House of Representatives and the Senate

constitution The written laws that govern a territory, state, or nation

context The circumstances or setting in which an event happens

correspondence Letters that are sent back and forth between people

credible Believable

culture The ideas, customs, and behaviors of a distinct people

document Something written or printed on paper

draft Mandatory recruitment for military service

economy Production and consumption of goods and services and the supply of money

Emancipation Proclamation A government order that freed the slaves in the Confederacy

embellish To make more interesting; to exaggerate

enslaved person A person who is owned by another, does not have any rights, and is treated as property

evidence The body of facts or information that proves that something is true or that an event took place

fascist A form of government in which a dictator and their political party have complete power over a country

federal Relating to a system of government in which several states form a country but can still make their own laws

historian A person who studies evidence from or about a particular time or event that has happened in the past

historical novel A book that attempts to portray a certain period in history

immigrants People coming into a country to live from another country

inauguration Formal admission of someone to a political position

independent Being free from the control of another person or nation

journalists People who write for newspapers or magazines

legitimate Legal or approved

lithograph A popular medium for artists in 1820 in which the artist draws an image on a smooth stone with a wax crayon or pencil; black ink is rolled over the finished image, and then paper is pressed against the stone to print the image. The artist then colors the print with paint.

memoir A personal story of one's life

parole In an army, release from duty or active service

patriotic Showing love or devotion for one's country

perspective Point of view

portrayed Shown or represented

primary sources Firsthand memories, accounts, documents, or artifacts from the past that serve as historical records about what happened at a particular time or event

revolution A time of great change; an uprising of the people to overthrow or change government, or gain independence

rout An overwhelming defeat

secede To leave an organization or nation

secession Act of withdrawing from a political state

secondary sources A historian's or artist's interpretations of primary sources

siege To surround an area, usually with a military force, and cut off supplies and communications coming in or going out

socialist A system in which the government, rather than citizens, owns and operates factories, farms, and businesses

society A group of people forming a single community with its own distinctive culture and institutions

source materials Original documents or other pieces of evidence related to a person, place, or event in history

Soviet Union A Union of 15 republics or states that included Russia and Ukraine, and which dissolved in 1991

telegrams Messages sent by telegraph and then written down or printed and delivered; telegraphy involves electrical signals passing along wires over long distances

tertiary Third in order

Union The northern states during the Civil War that stayed with the U.S. government

INDEX